POINTS OF VIEW

Should Students Have to Do COMMUNITY SERVICE?

By Amy B. Rogers

KidHaven PUBLISHING

Published in 2025 by
KidHaven Publishing, an Imprint of Greenhaven Publishing, LLC
2544 Clinton St.
Buffalo, NY 14224

Designer: Deanna Lepovich
Editor: Katie Kawa

Photo credits: Cover, p. 7 (top right) PeopleImages.com - Yuri A/Shutterstock.com; p. 5 Dmytro Zinkevych/Shutterstock.com; p. 7 (top left) SeventyFour/Shutterstock.com; p. 7 (bottom left) Krakenimages.com/Shutterstock.com; p. 7 (bottom middle) Nodar Gochashvili/Shutterstock.com; pp. 7 (bottom right), 9 Robert Kneschke/Shutterstock.com; p. 11 YAKOBCHUK VIACHESLAV/Shutterstock.com; p. 13 michaeljung/Shutterstock.com; p. 15 Arsenii Palivoda/Shutterstock.com; p. 17 Rawpixel.com/Shutterstock.com; p. 19 (left) wavebreakmedia/Shutterstock.com; p. 19 (right) Suzanne Tucker/Shutterstock.com; p. 21 (notepad) ESB Professional/Shutterstock.com; p. 21 (markers) Kucher Serhii/Shutterstock.com; p. 21 (photo frame) FARBAI/iStock/Thinkstock; p. 21 (inset, left) Photoroyalty/Shutterstock.com; p. 21 (inset, right) Kamira/Shutterstock.com.

Cataloging-in-Publication Data

Names: Rogers, Amy B.
Title: Should students have to do community service? / Amy B. Rogers.
Description: Buffalo, NY : KidHaven Publishing, 2025. | Series: Points of view | Includes glossary and index.
Identifiers: ISBN 9781534547766 (pbk.) | ISBN 9781534547773 (library bound) | ISBN 9781534547780 (ebook)
Subjects: LCSH: Service learning–Juvenile literature. | Helping behavior–Juvenile literature. | Voluntarism–Juvenile literature. | Community and school–Juvenile literature.
Classification: LCC LC220.5 R63 2025 | DDC 361.3’7–dc23

Printed in the United States of America

CPSIA compliance information: Batch #CSKH25: For further information contact Greenhaven Publishing LLC at 1-844-317-7404.

CONTENTS

A Helping HAND

Have you ever done something to help out in your community? Maybe you spent time cleaning up a park or beach. You might have taken part in a food or clothing drive, or you might have gone with your family to help serve food to those in need of a meal. These are all examples of community service.

Some schools require students to do community service. Many people believe this is good for both the community and the students. Others, though, believe community service shouldn't be mandatory, or required. What do you think?

Know the Facts!

Community service is also known as volunteering. This means doing something helpful because you want to do it. Volunteers don't get paid.

It's important to form your own educated, or informed, opinion on issues that could **affect** you, such as schools requiring community service. To have an informed opinion, you first need to learn the facts about the issue, so let's get started!

Many CHOICES

If schools require community service, students can often choose how they help out in their community. Choosing community service activities based on your interests can make volunteering fun—and it can even help you make new friends who share your interests.

For example, if you love animals, you could volunteer at a local animal **shelter**. If you love gardening, you could help take care of a community garden—or even start your own! If arts and crafts are fun for you, you could make cards to hand out at a local hospital or nursing home to brighten someone's day.

Know the Facts!

According to a volunteer organization, or group, called AmeriCorps, more than 60 million Americans volunteered with some kind of organization in 2021.

Schools often give students ideas and opportunities for community service activities. There are many ways to help make your community a better place!

Life LESSONS

With so many activities to choose from, people often believe community service teaches kids many lessons about the world beyond the classroom. Schools often require community service because school officials believe it gives students important learning **experiences** and helps them grow into active citizens and community members.

Many people who support mandatory community service do so because they believe it helps students become more **empathetic** and learn more about the world around them. Volunteer activities allow young people to learn about problems in their community, but they also allow young people to discover their own power to help.

Know the Facts!

Studies have shown that people who volunteer generally report feeling happier and having better overall **mental** health than people who don't volunteer.

Many people believe community service should be mandatory for students because it provides young people with hands-on experience in the real world. This is often seen as a valuable kind of learning that can't be done in the classroom.

Mandatory or VOLUNTARY?

Most people agree that there are many benefits to volunteering—for both the community and the person doing the community service. However, some people argue that many benefits of volunteering come from the fact that it's voluntary, or done by choice.

These people believe that if students are required to do community service, they'll see it as just another chore or more homework. This might make them less interested in helping others now and in the future. Instead, people who don't agree with mandatory community service say that students should be given more opportunities to choose to do community service.

Some people believe that if kids feel forced to do community service, they'll be less excited about helping others than they would be if they'd chosen to do it themselves. Many people, kids included, don't like doing things they're told they have to do.

Know the Facts!

Some U.S. states require students to perform a certain number of hours of community service to graduate, or finish school. In other states, each school district can make its own rules about community service. A school district is a group of public schools within one city, town, or part of a state.

College and BEYOND

Whether community service is required or done by choice, it can be very helpful for students. Many people support making community service mandatory for students, especially high school students, because it can help students get into good colleges. Colleges are often looking to accept students who've spent time helping their community.

Community service can also help students even before it's time to go to college. Some studies have shown that students who volunteer get better grades than students who don't. Many people believe the academic, or school-based, benefits of community service are a big reason why it should be mandatory.

People who support mandatory community service believe it helps students in school and even after they've graduated, or finished.

Know the Facts!

Volunteering can help people get jobs too. A group called the Corporation for National and Community Service found that people who've volunteered have almost a 30 percent better chance of being hired for a job than people who've never volunteered.

Too BUSY

Community service isn't the only thing colleges are looking for when deciding which students to accept. Good grades and **involvement** in after-school activities can also help students get into the colleges of their dreams. However, doing homework, studying hard, playing sports, and going to lessons for dance or music keep students very busy. It can be hard for them to find time to volunteer.

Some people believe students are already being pushed too hard and are too busy. They often argue that mandatory community service is just another **source** of **stress** for students instead of something that makes them feel good.

Know the Facts!

A 2022 study by the U.S. government showed that students today are more involved in sports and other after-school activities than they were 20 years ago.

When kids are too busy, it can cause problems with their sleep, their grades, and their health, especially their mental health.

Healthy and HAPPY

Some people believe community service can harm kids' mental health if those kids are already too busy. However, studies have shown that volunteering can help people's mental health. It can help people feel better about themselves and the world around them. It can also help them feel less stressed—even if they're still busy.

Another way community service can help someone's mental health is by allowing them to connect with others. Kids who volunteer can strengthen their social skills and make new friends by working with others on service projects, or activities, and tasks.

Community service projects often ask students to work with people they wouldn't otherwise meet in their everyday life. Many people believe this is an important life skill for students to have and a good argument for making community service mandatory.

Know the Facts!

Volunteering can help people stay **physically** healthy too. Many community service activities involve moving around, and moving the body helps keep it healthy. In addition, volunteering can reduce stress, which then reduces the chance of having health problems such as heart disease.

A Family ACTIVITY

Community service can sometimes be a family activity. Parents or guardians and their kids can volunteer together, and many people believe this is a good way for families to spend quality time together. However, it's not always easy for adults with jobs, housework, and children to care for to find time to volunteer.

Mandatory community service for students can sometimes be an added source of stress for parents and guardians. They often need to drive their children to community service opportunities. This can be hard when adults are already very busy.

Making community service mandatory for students doesn't just affect the students—it often affects the whole family. Because of this, many people believe volunteering should be a choice made with the whole family in mind. It can be stressful to add another activity to a busy family **schedule**—even if it's for a good cause!

Know the Facts!

A major study of family **transportation** showed that 38 percent of parents spend more than 5 hours each week driving their kids to school and other activities.

The Debate CONTINUES

As more schools continue to add community service requirements for their students, the **debate** about their value is sure to continue. Is it good to make kids volunteer in their community, or does that take away the choice to do good that makes volunteering so rewarding?

Now that you've learned more about arguments from people on both sides of this debate, it's time to ask yourself what you think. Remember to back up your opinion with facts, and respect people who may think differently. Everyone can have their own point of view!

Know the Facts!

Some schools offer service learning opportunities. This is a planned kind of volunteering that connects community service with things taught in the classroom.

Should students have to do community service?

YES

- Community service provides students with important lessons they can't learn in the classroom.
- Community service helps students grow into active, empathetic citizens.
- Community service activities can help students get into good colleges.
- Taking part in community service activities can help students' mental health and social skills.

NO

- Volunteering should be voluntary—otherwise it feels like more homework for students.
- Making community service mandatory makes students less excited about it and possibly less likely to volunteer as they get older.
- Mandatory community service can add extra stress to the lives of students who are already too busy.
- It can be hard for parents or guardians to find time to drive students to community service activities.

When comparing the two sides of a debate, it can be helpful to make a chart such as this one.

GLOSSARY

affect: To produce an effect on something.

debate: An argument or discussion about an issue, generally between two sides.

empathetic: Describing someone who is able to understand, be aware of, and feel another person's feelings and experiences.

experience: A life event. Also, skills or knowledge someone gets by doing something.

involvement: The act of taking part in.

mental: Relating to the mind.

physical: Relating to the body.

schedule: A list of times when certain events will happen or when certain things need to be done.

shelter: A place that offers food and housing for animals without a home.

source: A person, place, or thing from which something comes or where it can be found.

stress: A state of strong feelings of worry.

transportation: The act of moving people or things from one place to another.

For More INFORMATION

WEBSITES

Be a Volunteer

Kidshealth.org/en/kids/volunteering.html

This part of the KidsHealth website explains the benefits of volunteering for kids and gives examples of ways to serve in your community.

DoSomething.org

www.dosomething.org

This website offers young people tips for helping out in their community and making the world a better place.

BOOKS

Bell, Samantha. *12 Stories About Helping the Community*. Mankato, MN: 12 Story Library, 2020.

Chang, Kirsten. *Volunteering*. Minneapolis, MN: Bellwether Media, 2022.

Rossiter, Brienna. *Volunteering*. Lake Elmo, MN: Focus Readers, 2021.

INDEX